JOANNA
BO(.

THE UNTOLD STORY
OF JOANNA GAINES

TUSKER PRESS

Table of Content

Introduction

In addition to her work as a TV host, Joanna Gaines also runs her own business, designs interiors, writes books, and appears on HGTV. She and her husband, Chip Gaines, became household names thanks to their starring roles in the hit show Fixer Upper. The show was so popular that it continued for five years. Joanna and Spanky have renovated over 100 homes over the past 12 years. After seeing her work on the show, many people have grown to admire her distinct styles.

Joanna Gaines, the famous star of Fixer Upper, was born in Kansas on April 19, 1978. She's Nan and Jerry Stevens' middle child. Since our favorite designer's mother is Korean and her father is one-fourth German and one-quarter Lebanese, she is half Korean and half Caucasian. Joanna has a close relationship with her parents and respects them for sticking together through thick and thin. Joanna Gaines' parents must be incredibly pleased with her accomplishments.

Joanna had very supportive parents, but she still had a difficult upbringing. Because she was of mixed Asian and European ancestry, she was the target of cruel taunting. That was why she didn't have a big social circle. Her older sister, Teresa, and her younger sister, Mary Kay, made sure she never felt lonely. The Gaineses siblings were Joanna's closest confidantes. It appears that their relationship remains strong even today, based on her online profiles.

Moreover, Joanna has renovated the home for her younger sister Mary, whom she refers to as Mikey. Mikey, like Joanna, has a large, loving family. Their older sibling also hosts a YouTube show; her sister's is called Let's Talk with Teresa Ann. They all look out for and assist one another. Joanna is such a talented designer that you might assume she has formal training in the field. However, in 2001, she earned a bachelor's degree in communication from Baylor University. Joanna's career goal at the time was to write for a newspaper. Thus, she packed her bags and headed east to complete an internship in just two days.

Joanna's first job out of college was as an intern at a news magazine, but she quickly realized that journalism wasn't the path for her. She ultimately decided to return to Texas from New York because of this. Her first job in Texas was at the tire shop her dad owns. Although Joanna's father had hoped that she would take over the family business when he retired, she had other, more artistic ambitions.

Joanna Gaines is $10 million richer as a result of her decision to pursue a career as an interior designer. While she has achieved great success in business, she did not have an easy journey to the top. Both she and her husband had to start out from a lower economic position. Joanna needed to help support her husband financially, so she followed her passion and opened Magnolia Market, a store selling home furnishings, ornaments, and clothing accessories. The store was picking up momentum when she had to close it to focus on raising her two children.

Upon the store's closing, Joanna and Chip turned their attention to building and remodeling homes. In addition, she published her art on a blog accessible online. In 2013, after an HGTV executive saw their designs, the network offered them a show called Fixer Upper. The show was a hit for five seasons, and Joanna gained a legion of fans thanks to her outstanding talent and approachability. With an average of $30,000 per makeover, Joanna and Chip must have made at least $2.3 million from the 79 episodes.

The couple was also compensated by HGTV for their appearance, though the amount is unknown. They may have charged less in the first few seasons, but Joanna Gaines' salary surely increased as the show gained traction. Joanna and Chip's show ended in 2018 for a good reason. Many viewers who enjoyed watching them together were devastated by their decision. Their businesses, including Magnolia Homes, Magnolia Realty, Magnolia Market, Magnolia Seed & Supply, and Silos Baking Co., thrived even while they were away from the television industry.

Magnolia Homes is well-known for offering stylish furnishings and ornaments for the home. Similarly, Joanna and Chip's Magnolia Realty has become a go-to resource for people looking to buy one of their custom-designed and -built homes. And there are many places to eat and shop at The Magnolia Market in Silos, including the coffee shop Magnolia Press and the restaurant Magnolia Table. Magnolia Market's open setting is a major draw for vacationing families.

Joanna's pregnancy with her fifth child made it difficult for her to juggle her work and personal commitments at first. Joanna

Gaines's husband was a constant source of strength as she worked through this difficulty. In addition, Gaines, as the sole proprietor of the thriving Magnolia enterprise, undoubtedly brings in millions annually.

Joanna is a famous author and wealthy businesswoman. She has published several books detailing her life story and culinary expertise. In a book for young people, she has also written about bullying and self-esteem. Joanna and her husband haven't watched television in almost three years. But now they have their own TV network, called Magnolia Network. There are 12 shows on this channel so far, and they cover topics like cooking, gardening, and health and fitness. Even more, Joanna will make appearances on a few of the programs. Everyone is itching for them to return to television.

After receiving such positive fan feedback, the channel has a good chance of becoming established and thriving in the years to come. Joanna Gaines's wealth will rise in the coming days as a direct result of the success of their network. Joanna and Chip Gaines tied the knot on

May 31, 2003. In fact, they first crossed paths when Joanna was working in her father's tire shop. This couple has been happily married for 18 years despite the fact that their personalities couldn't be more different. In many interviews, Joanna Gaines' husband has been quoted as saying, **Jo (Joanna) keeps me grounded.**

Joanna and her family have been residing in a farm house in Waco, Texas, since 2012. Not only that, but the adorable couple has a total of five children: three sons and two daughters. Drake Gaines, son of Chip and Joanna, was born on May 4, 2004. Then, on October 23, 2006, Ella Gaines was born. Two years later, on May 23, 2008, their third child, Duke Gaines, was born. After that, on February 1, 2010, their fourth daughter, Emmie Kay Gaines, was born, and on June 23, 2018, their youngest son, Crew Gaines, entered the world.

Joanna and Chip are strict parents because they only let their kids use the iPads for a set amount of time each week. They value modesty and originality in their offspring. And yet, Joanna Gaines' kids have it pretty good. It's a testament to Joanna's motherly abilities that she still finds time to run such a successful business. Joanna and her husband are growing their company and their reputation with each passing day. We're rooting for them to take over the industry like they have with Fixer Upper. We wish the best of luck to our favorite duo.

Chapter One

Early Life

On April 19, 1978, Joanna Gaines was born. She was born in Waco, a city in the state of Texas, in the country of the United States of America. She was born in the United States, and her astrological sign is Aries. Teresa Criswell, her older sister, hosts the Let's Talk With Teresa Ann series on YouTube, which is part of the Inspiration channel.

As Joanna Gaines grew older, she helped her father manage the family's tire store. As a result, her father taught her a lot about the organization. She was able to gain skills and experience in a variety of retail settings, allowing her to graduate. One of her other siblings is named Mary Kay McCall. Jerry Stevens, her father, is of Lebanese and German descent, and her mother, Nan Stevens, is of Korean descent. Jerry Stevens is half-German and half-Lebanese.

Chapter Two

Joanna Gaines' Education

Joanna went to Baylor University and graduated (her husband, Chip, also attended Baylor). Despite the fact that she appears to have a design degree, this is not the case. Joanna majored in communications during her undergraduate studies. Her initial ambition was to pursue a career in the field of communications. Joanna worked as an intern for the television show with Dan Rather in New York City while she was a student at Baylor University, according to Baylor

Magazine. Despite the fact that she was well on her way to a successful career in communications, Joanna decided to take a different path. She quickly realized she had a natural talent for design. Joanna found that going to different stores in New York City gave her new ideas for her business.

Joanna was bullied in school

Joanna told Darling magazine that she was picked on and felt insecure as a child. She explained in an interview that if people thought she was confident, it was really just a way for her to hide her insecurity because she didn't want people to get to know the real her. She said, in case you haven't already heard, that her mother is entirely Korean and her father is Caucasian. She said when she was in kindergarten, the other kids teased her because she was Asian. You don't really know how to process something like that at that age. She said her interpretation of who she was was that she was not good enough.

Gaines discovered that she was unable to reach out to people and make new friends when she transferred to a new high school as a sophomore. She explained that her fear and insecurities just took over, and as a result, she found herself eating lunch alone in the restroom. Gaines later struggled with her identity and sense of self-worth when she moved to New York during her senior year of college. She said she realized her purpose was to help people who are insecure because she didn't like how it made her feel in that stall; she explained that's not who she was. She added that she didn't like how it made her feel in there.

She is currently expecting her fifth child with her husband and co-star Chip, and she believes that her time alone shaped the kind of parent she is today.

She told Darling that she always tells her kids to look for the kid on the playground who isn't playing with anyone, to go reach out, ask them their name, to look for the kid in the lunchroom who isn't sitting with anyone, and be their friend. She said that she thinks that when you come from a place like that, even if it was only for six months, there's always that place of humility *you never want to forget. She said that the experience grounded her in the fact that she wants to look for the lonely, the sad, and the people who aren't confident, because that's not where they're supposed to stay.*

Chapter Three

Career -Big Business

In addition to being the editor-in-chief of The Magnolia Journal, her magazine that launched in the fall of 2016, Joanna Gaines is also the author of At Home: A Blog by Joanna Gaines. Her most recent book is We Are Gardeners, a children's book she wrote with her kids about gardening, but she has also written several others about cooking, interior design, and other topics. In the fall of last year, she and Joanna Gaines finished their third season of working together on

Matilda Jane Clothing, an adorable line of clothing for children. Plus, she and her husband are raising their five young children on a working farm in Texas.

Joanna and Chip Gaines are business partners in a number of different ventures: the Magnolia Homes construction and design firm seen on their popular show; the Magnolia Table restaurant; the Magnolia Kids children's furniture store; Magnolia Realty, which serves multiple cities in Texas; their magazine, The Magnolia Journal; and the Magnolia Market, housed in the remodeled Magnolia Silos in Waco (and online at magnolia.com). They also make the Hearth and Hand brand, which sells well at Target stores across the country.

The Road Back to TV

Joanna's recently announced return to television, however, must rank among the most important events on her agenda. Joanna and Chip revealed their plans to return to television in November on The Tonight Show Starring Jimmy Fallon; their spokesman, John Marsicano, later confirmed the news to PEOPLE. According to Marsicano, preliminary discussions about a lifestyle-focused media network for Magnolia have begun with Discovery. She said they hope to build a different kind of platform for unique, inspiring, and family-friendly content together, but the specifics of this opportunity are still being worked out. Since HGTV is also owned by Discovery Inc., the new venture won't be too far from the original television homes of the two.

Living Beyond Dreams

Why do so many fans crave more Joanna Gaines content? Because her genuineness shines through to her readers and viewers, they feel a genuine connection to her as a person rather than a celebrity. Everything she does is infused with her whole being. Her adoring audience can sense her devotion to each and every one of her customers, relatives, and businesses. She is soothing, steady, and in charge, and her example encourages other women to believe in themselves and their abilities.

Joanna said on Magnolia.com that this whole business idea was born completely out of a dream she didn't know could ever come to life. Her very loyal, brave, and brave-hearted husband was the reason she went after what she loved.

Finding the Balance

But seriously, how does the mother of five get everything done? Over the years, Joanna has shared advice that has contributed to her success as a mother and businesswoman. The Money & Career section of the lifestyle website CheatSheet® is the source of some of these suggestions:

Don't compartmentalize motherhood from business ownership. She includes her kids in her work by asking for their input on things like paint color choices and even taking them on business trips with her and her husband.

Do your best to participate. You have to give it your all to your job and your family, she says, in order to be happy in both areas. She gives it her all at work and at home with her loved ones.

Priorities should be with one's family. She gives her projects her full attention while she's working on them, but she insists that family comes first. She said that the balance thing is hard because, at first, that's what she was trying to do and she was kind of going crazy.

It's important to strike a balance between work and play so that life doesn't feel like one long, relentless grind. Joanna thinks the outdoor activities she and her family enjoy provide a welcome respite from their hectic schedules. Her children are essential components of her gardening and livestock raising endeavors, which serve as a means of relaxation and family bonding for the whole family.

If you have to spend time away from your children, remember that you are setting a good example for them by working hard. She believes her children are learning the importance of hard work and what it takes to succeed because of the example she is setting for them. She explains that she has to work because her children also need to attend school.

Recognize your weaknesses and those of your team, and play to their strengths. It's smart to ask for assistance in areas that aren't your forte from those you trust. Recognizing that Chip is better at putting their kids to sleep by swaddling and rocking them is a simple way to reduce stress.

A closed door always has a corresponding open one. Although Joann's original goal was to open a store like Magnolia Market, she had to give it up early on so that she and Chip could concentrate on building their real estate business, Magnolia

Homes. In light of the overwhelming response to the reopening of Magnolia Market following the tremendous success of Magnolia Homes and associated businesses, the original location has been significantly expanded. Similarly, the announcement of their fifth pregnancy confirmed their decision to end their popular show Fixer Upper, freeing them up to consider even more exciting opportunities. Joanna has learned that it's okay to back off, change directions, or reimagine her goals along the way.

Chapter Five

Personal life

Chip and Joanna Gaines' Relationship timeline

The Gaines have been a couple for 18 years and have made quite a name for themselves in that time. The Fixer Upper series on HGTV was the first step in what has become a full-fledged home improvement empire for the husband-and-wife team. They have since published multiple books, created a line of home accessories for Target, and launched their own television network. They've also raised five kids together, which is no small feat. So it's not surprising that their love story is intriguing. a look back at their relationship, from the beginning to the present.

2001: Initial Get Together

The two initially crossed paths at a car shop in Waco, Texas. Chip once visited Joanna's father's store and noticed a family portrait behind the counter. According to Popsugar, he stated that the picture on the wall convinced him that he would marry her one day.

Chip told KWTX that his buddies used to always joke that no one could get their brakes done as often as he got his brakes done. Chip made several trips back to the shop in an effort to meet Joanna. It was when Chip went in to get his brakes fixed and Joanna was working in the office that the two finally met. Joanna claims they hit it off immediately after meeting each other in the waiting room.

2001: First Date

The two went on their first date not long after they first met, and it did not go as either of them had hoped. They wrote about their first date in their memoir, The Magnolia Story. When Chip was 90 minutes late to pick her up, Joanna wrote in an excerpt for Today that she was prepared to cancel entirely. When he arrived, however, everything altered.

She said she couldn't put a finger on what he said that made her agree to go with him. She wrote that he hadn't even prepared for their date. When he finally arrived, he made no mention of his tardiness. His self-assurance was absolutely astounding. She said she couldn't say for sure. This is something she just doesn't understand. No one would be upset by Chip's 1.5-hour tardiness, but they still wouldn't wait for him.

The date went well, but it took Chip a few months to finally call Joanna to set up another one. Here's an excerpt from The Magnolia Story in which he reveals that he and a friend once made a bet to see who could wait the longest before calling their dates back. He explained in his letter that he was hoping that John would give him the fifty dollars.

That's why he didn't call back, anyhow.

2002: Engagement

After dating for about a year, Chip finally proposed. An excerpt from The Magnolia Story was featured on the website Cosmopolitan, and it reveals that Chip lied to Joanna by saying they were attending a private concert. To avoid this, he took her to a mall, proposed, and then had an engagement ring custom-made. They went out to dinner to celebrate their engagement, and Joanna wrote that her parents, her little sister, Chip's parents, and his sister were all there waiting to celebrate their engagement with them.

May 31, 2003: Wedding in Texas

Joanna has said that the historic Earle Harrison House in Waco, Texas, where the couple got married, looks just like the house where they went on their first date.

2003: First house flip

Joanna began assisting Chip in house flipping shortly after they were married, and they made their first purchase as a married couple shortly thereafter. Joanna said to Popsugar that she could remember the smell, referring to the time they began renovating their home after returning from their honeymoon. The house was terrible. Chip performed all the construction work; She added that she can still picture him staining floors and laying tiles late into the night.

October 16, 2003: Opening Magnolia Market

After that successful flip, the two launched another aspect of their business: the Magnolia Market. After the fact, Joanna expressed her appreciation to the 40 patrons who came in that day in an Instagram post. She said she was extremely grateful for the customers who came in that day to support them. Joanna mentioned opening a retail shop as a lifelong goal in an interview with Baylor University, saying that for 10 years, she had a notebook where she would write all her dreams and other business ideas. Before they got married, Chip told her that she should make one of those things happen.

2004-2010: Domestic Expansion

After that, for the next seven years, they put all of their energy into growing their family and their company. Their first child, a son named Drake, was born on May 4, 2004. Their first daughter, Ella Rose, was born on October 23, 2006. Their second son, Duke, was born on May 23, 2008, and their second daughter, Emmie Kay, was born on February 1, 2010.

They decided to shut down Magnolia Market in 2005 and

convert the space into the Magnolia Homes headquarters, where they could focus on real estate, home renovation, and interior design. Chip told the students at Baylor University that they had to learn to work together, and that has really helped to forge a solid marriage that has served them well not only in business but in life.

May 23, 2013: The Show Begins

The Gaines' rise to fame was hastened by the premiere of Fixer Upper, the HGTV hit that attracted an average of 1.9 million viewers per episode. Later, in an interview with Popsugar, Joanna said that she always dreamed of the idea of television but never thought it would have to do with design or renovations.

October 2015: The Grand Opening of Yet Another Store

Both of them returned to the retail sector not long after the first season of Fixer Upper aired. They launched Magnolia Market at the Silos, a commercial hub with numerous stores and eateries. In 2016, up to 35,000 people per week visited the complex, as reported by Texas Monthly.

These two have discussed the challenges of working in such close quarters. For example, Joanna told People that early on, they had their fair share of fights and figured out where the boundaries were. She said he has a firm grasp on the big picture and is a capable risk assessor. She enjoys the finer points.

2016: More business launches

As a result of the popularity of Fixer Upper and Magnolia Market at the Silos, 2016 was a monumental year *for the Gaineses. They came out with a set of home decor items, including paint hues, wallpaper patterns, and furniture. They also released the first issue of their quarterly lifestyle magazine, The Magnolia Journal, and opened a bed and breakfast called The Magnolia House.*

The Magnolia Story, their first book written together, came out that same year. They chronicled the high points of their relationship and shared intimate details of their lives together in a book. Joanna stated that one pretty amazing thing they learned early on was that the more time we spent together, the better their relationship was, which was taken from their book and posted on their blog.

She went on to say that they appear to give each other energy. Neither of them has ever felt the need to separate from the other because of how well they work together. She said that they have had their share of setbacks and disagreements, but that they have always been committed to facing their problems as a couple.

August 2017: Divorce Rumors

Even though Chip and Joanna's marriage appeared to be thriving, rumors of a possible split surfaced in 2017. One of Chip's followers tweeted that they were getting tired of the stories, to which he replied that it wouldn't ever happen! That is a guarantee—100 percent! with the hashtag #loveofmylife.

September 2017: The End of Fixer Upper?

Chip and Joanna's shocking announcement that Season 5 of Fixer Upper would be the show's last came as a shock to viewers. Their marriage and family life were praised in an online post with the words, that their family is healthy. And that people should disregard the rumors about a phony skincare line and everything else they've read thus far; that it was completely unrelated.

They are just pausing to acknowledge that they're exhausted. Their plan was to use this time to focus on their family and their businesses, giving them the care and attention they deserved while also addressing any areas of weakness.

At roughly the same time, the couple announced that they would be collaborating with Target on a home and lifestyle brand called Hearth & Hand with Magnolia.

2018 January 2: A Major Announcement

Their decision to start a family in 2018 came as another shock to their adoring public. Chip captioned a photo of himself and Joanna comparing their baby bumps with, Gaines' party of 7. (If you're still confused.. WE ARE PREGNANT) @joannagaines.

February 26, 2018: A New Restaurant

After the announcement, the couple had more news to start the New Year: they had opened a restaurant called Magnolia Table. Some of the vegetables and eggs used at Joanna's restaurant in Waco, Texas, which specializes in breakfast, come from her own garden.

June 23, 2018: Crew Gaines Is Born

Joanna announced the birth of her son at the beginning of the summer by posting a photo of the two of them together in the hospital. She gushed that they were so in love with their new baby boy, Crew Gaines. Because he was such a pleasant surprise from the start, he arrived in the world two and a half weeks early. She said that they appreciate people's prayers and positive energy. They are truly appreciative.

April 2019: A New Media Company

Chip and Joanna showed in 2019 that the birth of their fifth son wasn't going to slow them down professionally. In a press release, Discovery, Inc., and Magnolia announced the formation of a multiplatform media joint venture. The name **Magnolia Network** comes from this development.

August 2020: A Big Reboot

When it was announced that Chip and Joanna Gaines would be bringing back Fixer Upper, viewers rejoiced. Chip told Deadline that for the past few years, they've continued taking on renovations and projects, doing the work they are passionate about, but he doesn't think either of them anticipated how the show would become such a permanent fixture in their hearts.

June 2021: Anniversary Celebrations

It was in June that Chip and Joanna marked 18 years of marriage. Joanna captioned the touching Instagram video tribute with photos from their time together. She said she was grateful for the opportunity to share this journey with him and wished themselves a happy anniversary.

They had an interview with Oprah Winfrey at the time for her Super Soul Sunday special, where they discussed how their relationship brings out the best in each other.

In August 2022, Gaines announced she was releasing her first solo memoir.

Joanna included a heartfelt caption about the book's origins and the creative process behind its cover design. Joanna posted a picture of the final version of the manuscript for her book along with a caption that explained what it was about.

She revealed that she began jotting down memories and stories from the past earlier this year and that she was still trying to work through these things in her journal years later. Further, she said that half of her life is behind her, and she has been longing for clarity about what she should carry forward and how she could hold this next chapter well. At some point, she said, she realized she was telling a story—her story. She explained that she was made up of all these different pieces.

She continued that it was complicated, winding, and lovely, and it generously unveiled a thousand marvels. She said that it both tore at her heart and helped mend it in unexpected ways.

She said she took this picture the day she finished it, and today they sent it off to the printer!! She exclaimed that it was no longer in her control; now was the time to disseminate it.

She went on to say that she was experiencing a wide range of emotions, from nervousness to excitement to apprehension to vulnerability to hope. Joanna prayed that the light of her story might somehow illuminate the darkness of yours.

Joanna also mentioned that the #TheStoriesWeTell can be preordered through the profile link.

Controversies

biggest controversy over the years

Some individuals seem to be destined for fame. They have the ideal combination of uncommon skill and endearing charm—just the components needed to lure people in and keep them engaged. Just ask HGTV, which found the Texas-based home-improvement couple Chip and Joanna Gaines. The two made their television debut in 2013 with Fixer

Upper, when they demonstrated their talent for converting obviously inhospitable rooms into dream houses. Chip and Joanna were an immediate fan favorite, and they quickly became household names.

By its sixth season, Fixer Upper was averaging 19.6 million viewers per week, making it one of HGTV's most-watched series. On the heels of their meteoric success, Chip and Joanna developed a retail marketplace, authored a best-selling book, and established a slew of lifestyle companies. In addition, on July 15, 2021, they launched their own network, Magnolia, in collaboration with Discovery, Inc. They've undoubtedly developed a booming enterprise in just eight years.

However, their path to success—and multimillionaire status—has not been without hiccups. While popularity has its advantages, being in the public spotlight has also exposed Chip and Joanna to heightened scrutiny and criticism, whether it's for their religious beliefs or their parenting. They've also had to deal with a few legal squabbles along the way. Even this endearing television duo is not immune to controversy. Let us investigate more.

Their dubious church affiliation

In a 2016 BuzzFeed post, the Gaineses' religious allegiance garnered harsh criticism. It's hardly surprising that the couple are religious. People have taken issue with the church they attend and its dubious teachings towards the LGBTQIA+ community.

According to the media outlet, their church, Antioch Community Church, is a nondenominational, evangelical, mission-based megachurch. And their pastor, Jimmy Seibert, who recently referred to the Gaineses as **close friends** in a video, is adamantly opposed to same-sex marriage and advocates for LGBT people to be converted to straight. Although the pair did not publicly state that they believed and accepted the church's position on the matter,

Collaboration with Target

Because Joanna and Chip have religious links, their fan group was outraged when they announced a relationship with Target in 2017.

While some customers were ecstatic to be able to bring some of their trendy décor items into their own homes, many others were disappointed that they opted to collaborate with Target.

Hearth & Hand Magnolia, their Target line, ruffled some feathers. Many conservative fans rushed to social media to complain about the Gaineses' decision to do business with Target, which lets transgender customers and staff use the fitting rooms and restrooms that best match their gender identity.

Vacation Rentals for Fixer Upper Homes

People who were fortunate enough to have the pair work on their property wanted to cash in, according to the Waco Tribune-Herald, since the couple's Fixer Upper program primarily focused on residences in Waco, Texas. The owners of almost half a dozen residences restored by the Gaineses were listed on online property rental sites VRBO (Vacation Rentals by Owner) and Airbnb, much to Chip and Joanna's chagrin. And these owners were attracting a lot of attention because of their residences' links to reality TV personalities.

After all of this was revealed, the pair made a significant move, altering how they chose display candidates for a home remodel. Brock Murphy, a Magnolia spokeswoman, said in a statement that they are going to be more stringent with their contracts regarding Fixer Upper clients going forward.

She said they wish to thank the national television viewers. They wish to modify people's houses. That is the fundamental aim of their program, and they want to make sure it is not forgotten in the midst of this new vacation rental craze.

Chip's former business partners filed a lawsuit against him.

Chip owns Magnolia Realty in addition to his TV business. He founded the business with two buddies, Richard Clark and John Lewis, but it failed about the time Chip became well-known on television. When Chip and Joanna signed their HGTV contract, the two *partners were convinced to sell their stakes in the firm. And they didn't make much money when they sold their stock. To make matters worse, the business partners had no idea Chip had a major HGTV deal lined up. So, in 2017, Clark and Lewis sued Chip, claiming fraud and seeking $1 million in damages.*

In a suit filed on behalf of Clark and Lewis, attorney David Tekell wrote that at a time when only the defendants knew that Fixer Upper had been fast-tracked for a one-hour premiere on HGTV and was about to radically change their lives and businesses, Chip Gaines plotted to get rid of his business partners, despite their longtime friendship, to make sure that he alone would profit from Magnolia Realty's connection with Fixer Up.

Chip addressed the problem on social media in April 2017 in a carefully disguised and passive-aggressive tweet, writing, for the record, he have had the same mobile phone number for the last 15 years. For the last 20 years, he has used the same email address. No one called or sent you an email? Four years later, friends' file a lawsuit. He said he was clearly portraying his erstwhile partners as nothing more than opportunists.

Resentment among homeowners

In 2017, the owners of a Waco home that Joanna and Chip worked on during season three of Fixer Upper said they were duped by the program when a guy accused of drunk driving broke through their front wall. The owners claimed they were tricked into accepting the property by the Gaines and the program in the first place. Evidently, they found their new area unwelcoming, insecure, and noisy after moving in.

The pair told the Waco Tribune-Herald it's like the Wild West here. The bars and the businesses across the street have been causing quite a stir. It's been an issue from the beginning. They have been here for a year and a half and feel duped by Waco and Magnolia Realty.

Parking Issues

According to the Waco Tribune-Herald, a neighbor of Chip and Joanna's Magnolia Market complex in Waco was planning to charge shoppers $10 to park in his lot, which was just next door, in 2017. In response, Chip erected a fence to warn clients that they could not park there. The owner of the adjoining property alleged in a lawsuit that the gate prohibited foot and vehicle access to his company. As a consequence, he filed a $1 million lawsuit against Chip and Joanna. Instead of pursuing the case, the Gaineses finally purchased the land.

Lead paint violations by the EPA

Chip and Joanna's firm was fined in 2018 for breaking the Environmental Protection Agency's lead paint limits. According to Vox, older houses in numerous seasons of the program did not reflect "lead-safe labor techniques" and breached restrictions on dangerous chemicals and lead paint. The EPA claims that the couple's firm violated the Lead Renovation, Repair, and Painting Rule (RRP Rule) and the Toxic Substances Control Act (TSCA) in 33 Waco houses it refurbished. Also, the information shows that the group hired to remove the lead paint did not do it in a safe way.

The show's production firm was fined $40,000 and ordered to spend $160,000 to clean up lead pollution in the Waco neighborhood. It was also decided that the program's hosts would have to discuss lead paint safety on their show and on social media. Chip has issued a few safety alerts on Twitter since then, including one in 2018 that said that during last night's program, several folks had worries regarding remodeling properties with suspected lead-based paint. He followed up with a link to a directory of qualified renovators.

The Gaineses were chastised for their parenting.

Chip and Joanna have a lot on their plates with their busy occupations and five children. When the couple only had four children, writer Daryl Austin penned a post for USA Today criticizing them for putting their enterprises ahead of their children. Chip was irritated by the criticism, so he retaliated. In 2018, Chip tweeted that he doesn't know Daryl, and he definitely doesn't *know him. For the record, if there is ever a need with his family (1st), he will shut down the circus so quickly that his head will spin. It's unclear whether Austin was forced to retract his statements or if he truly regretted what he said, but he later wrote an apology to the Gaineses, expressing regret for writing what he did about the couple and how they raise their children.*

Printed in Great Britain
by Amazon

14853495R00047